MW01133411

ARABIC LETTERS
PRACTICE FOR BEGINNERS

تعلم الحروف
العربية

This Book Belongs To:

....

....

الحروف العربية
Arabic Letters

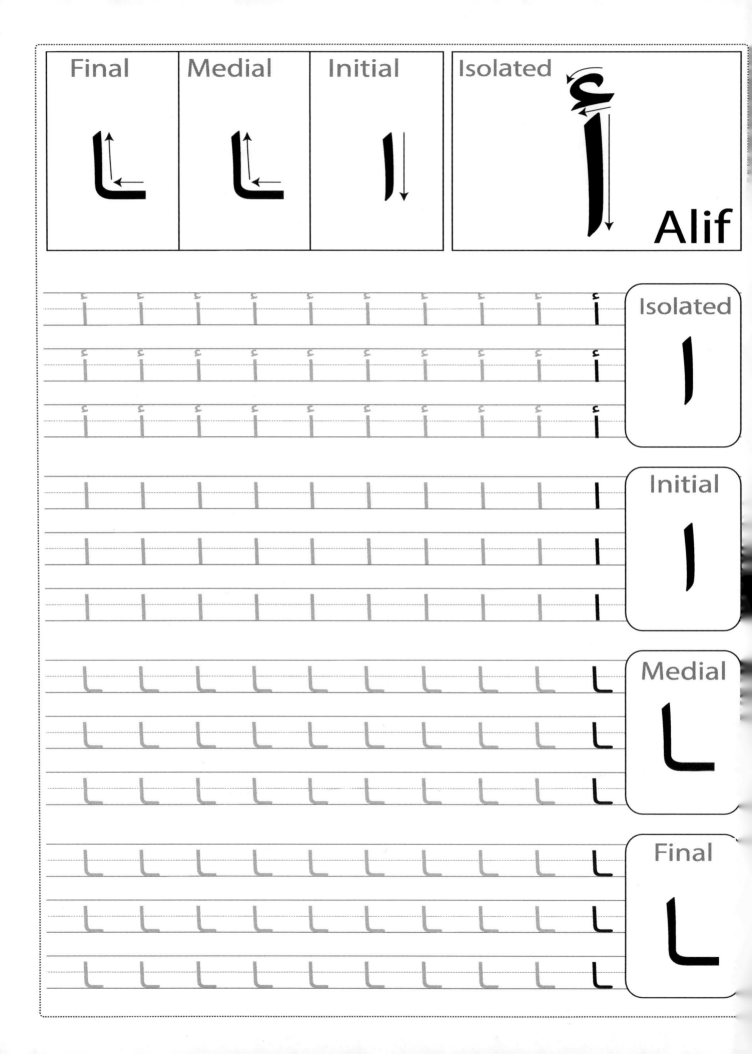

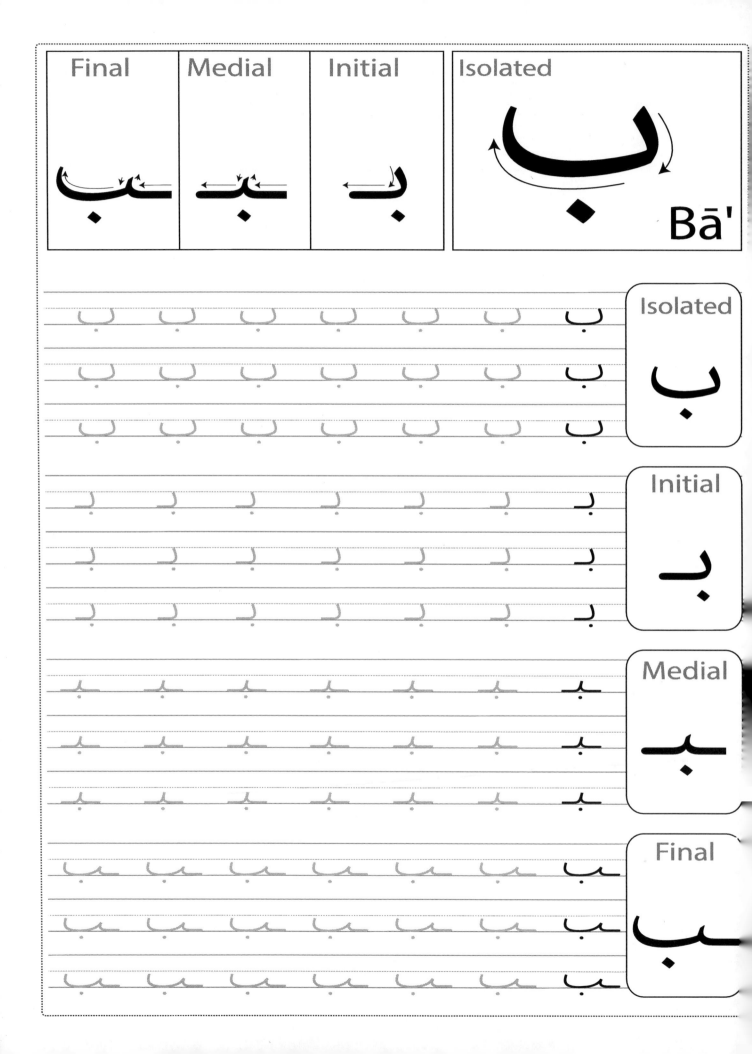

Final	Medial	Initial	Isolated

Bā'

Isolated

ب

Initial

بـ

Medial

ـبـ

Final

ـب

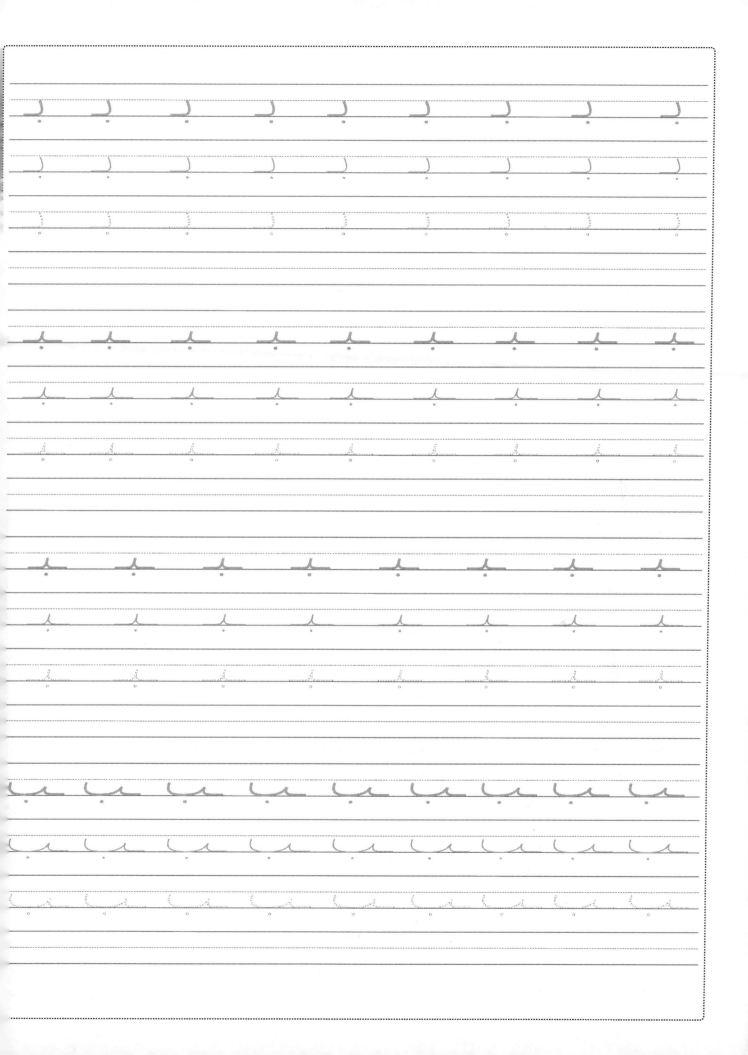

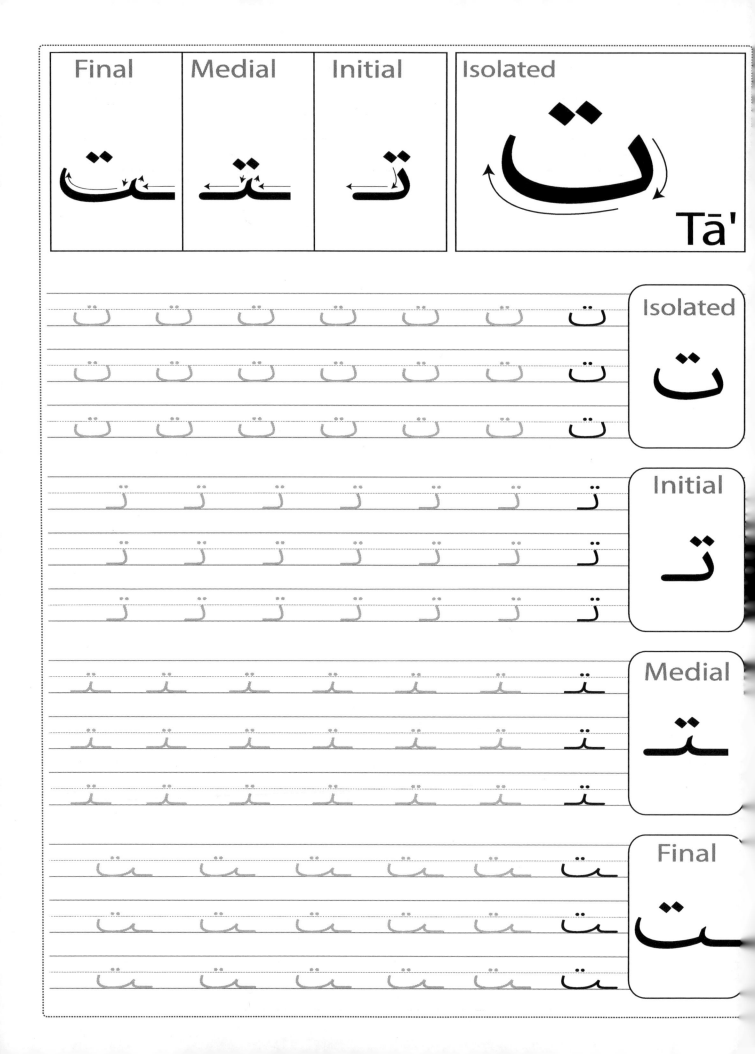

Final	Medial	Initial	Isolated
ـت	ـتـ	تـ	ت

Tāʼ

Isolated — ت

Initial — تـ

Medial — ـتـ

Final — ـت

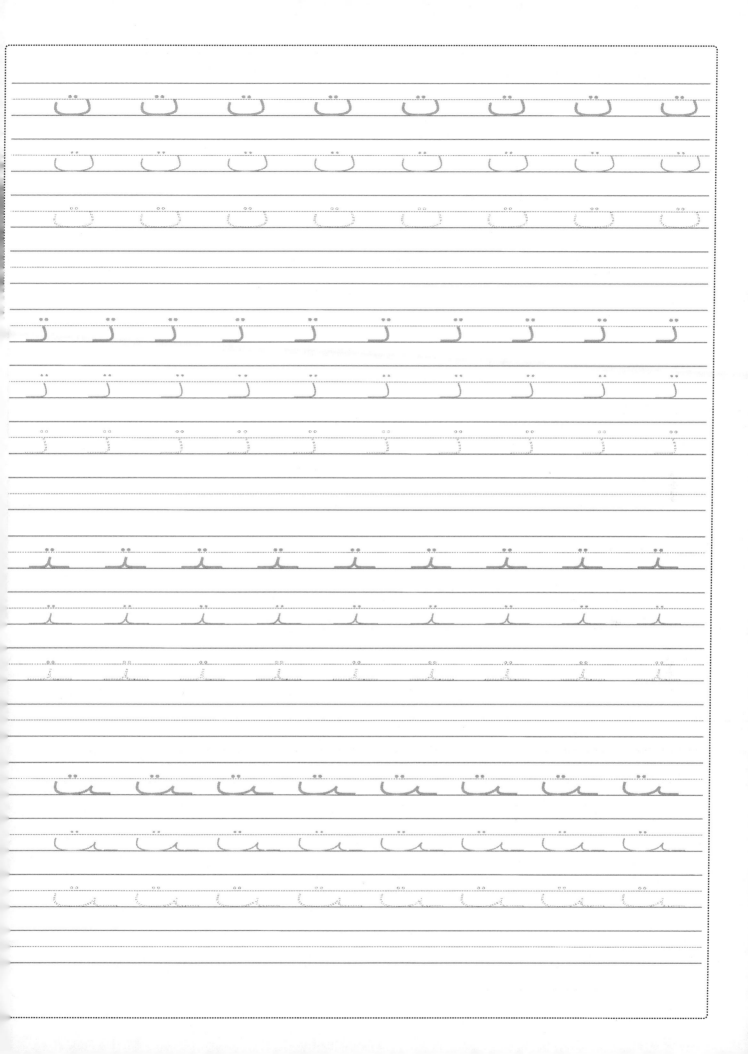

Final	Medial	Initial	Isolated
ـث	ـثـ	ثـ	ث Thā'

Isolated — ث

Initial — ثـ

Medial — ـثـ

Final — ـث

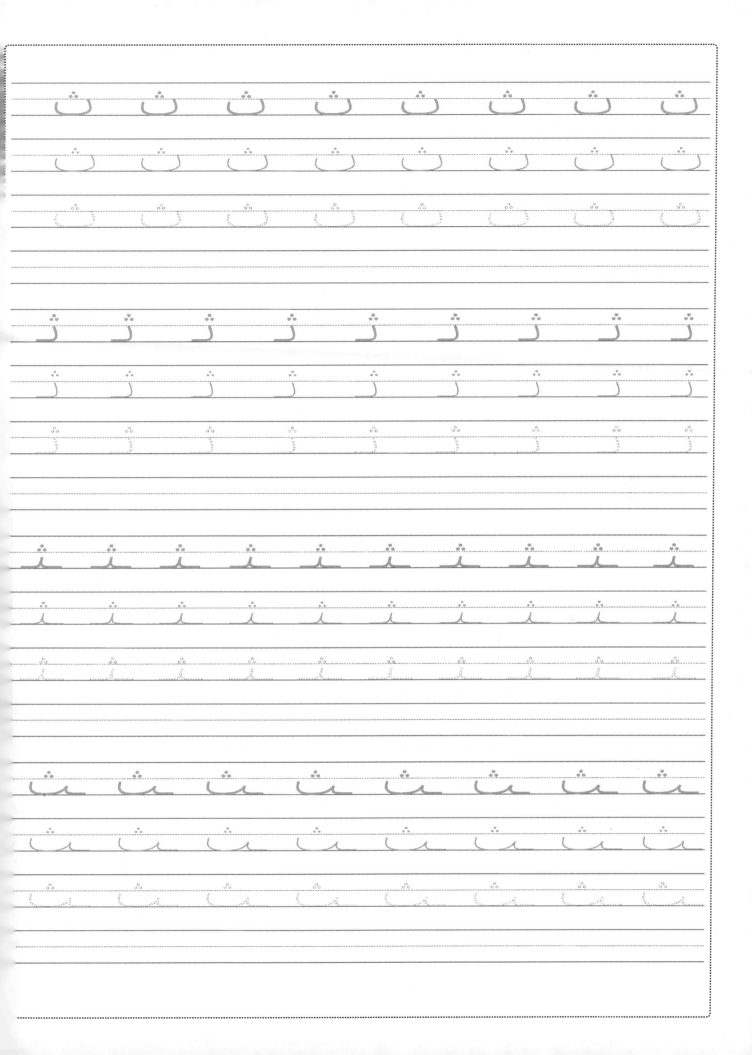

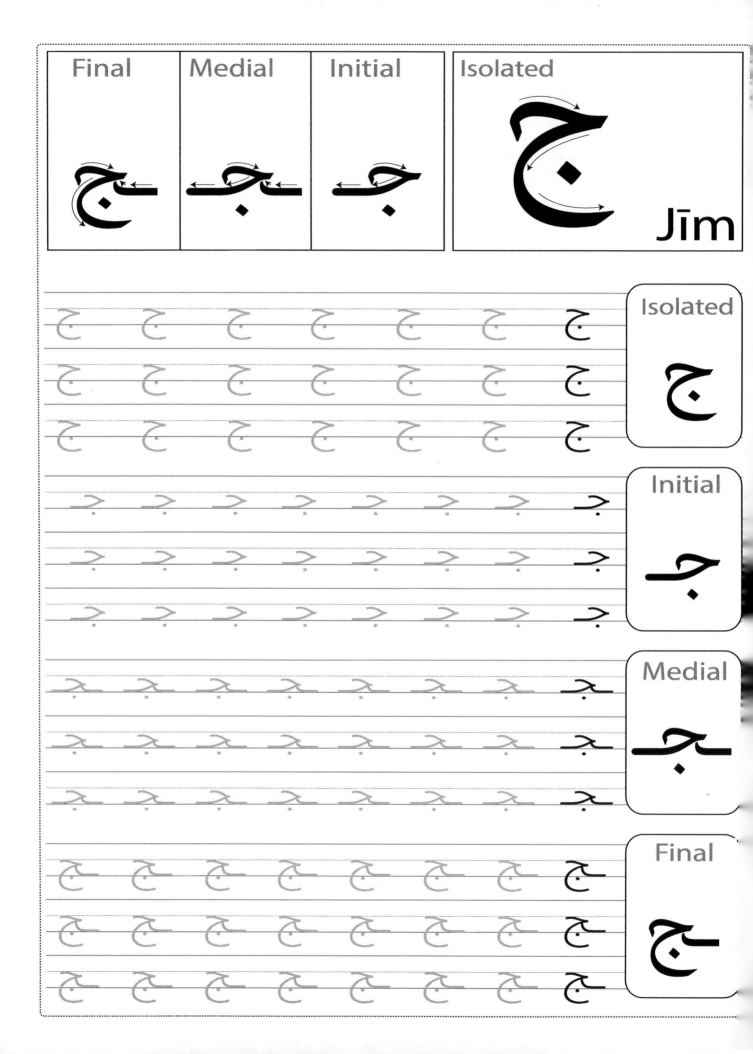

Final	Medial	Initial	Isolated

Jīm

Isolated

Initial

Medial

Final

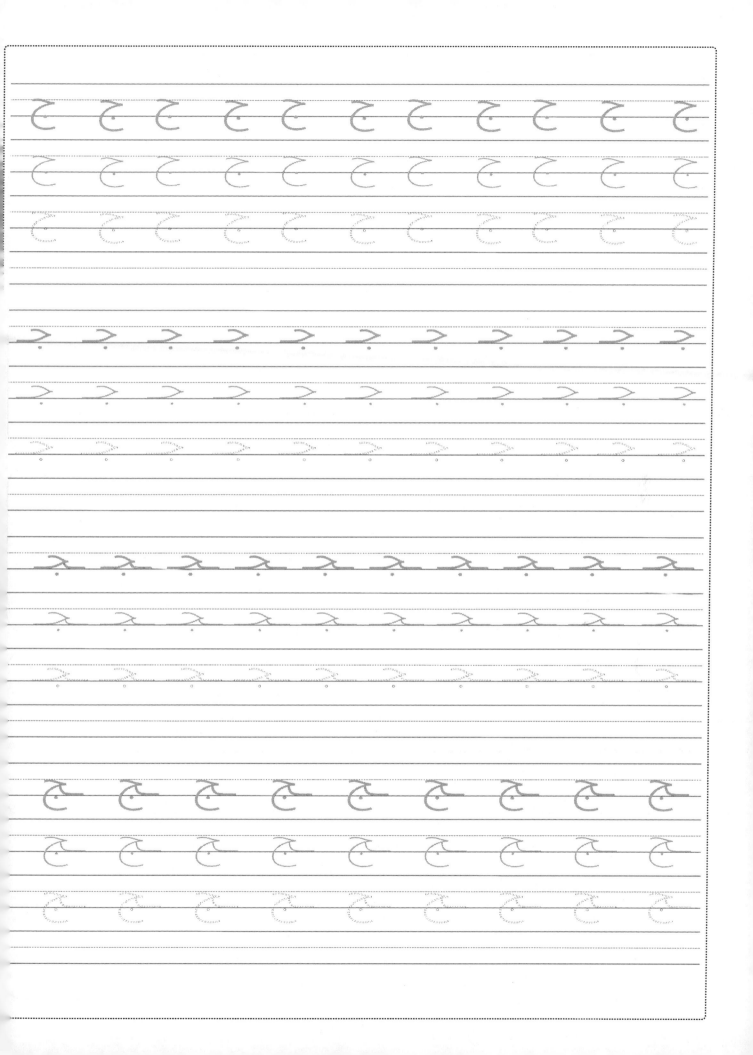

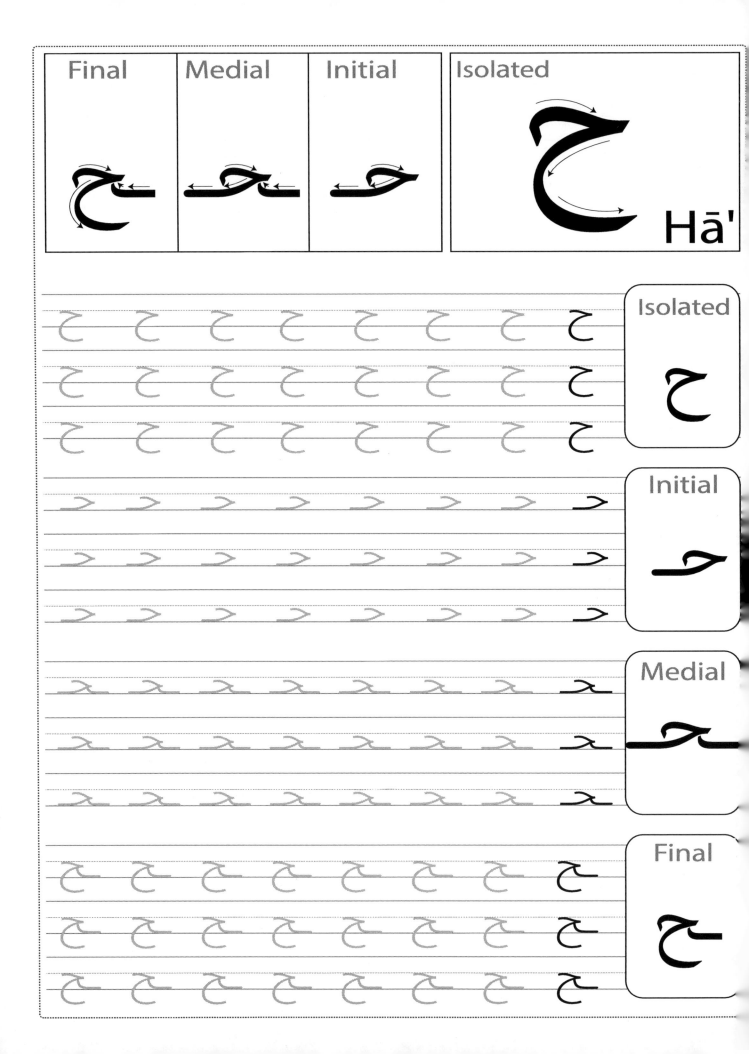

Final	Medial	Initial	Isolated

Hā'

Isolated

Initial

Medial

Final

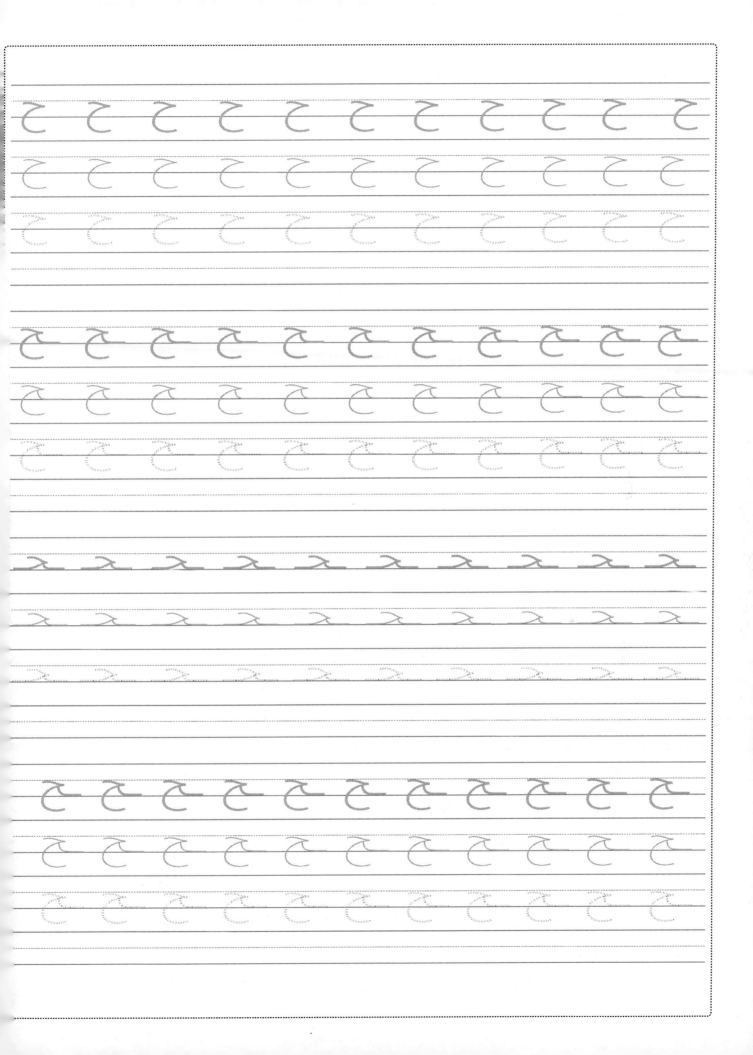

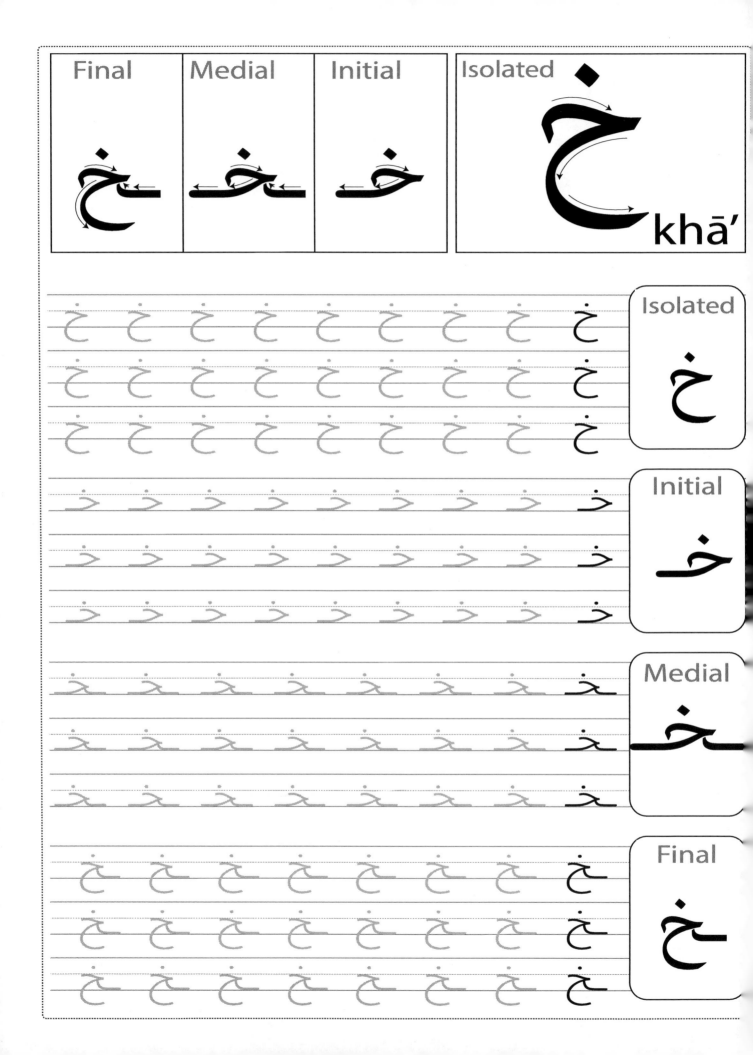

Final	Medial	Initial	Isolated ◆

khā'

| | Isolated |
| | خ |

| | Initial |
| | خ |

| | Medial |
| | خ |

| | Final |
| | خ |

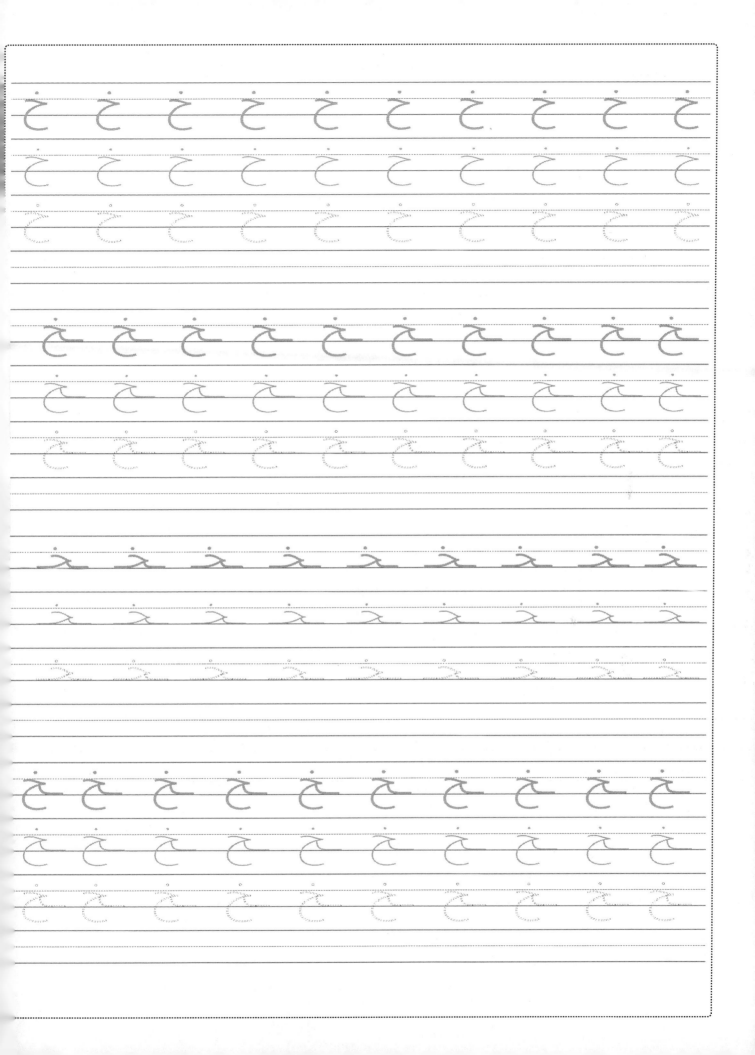

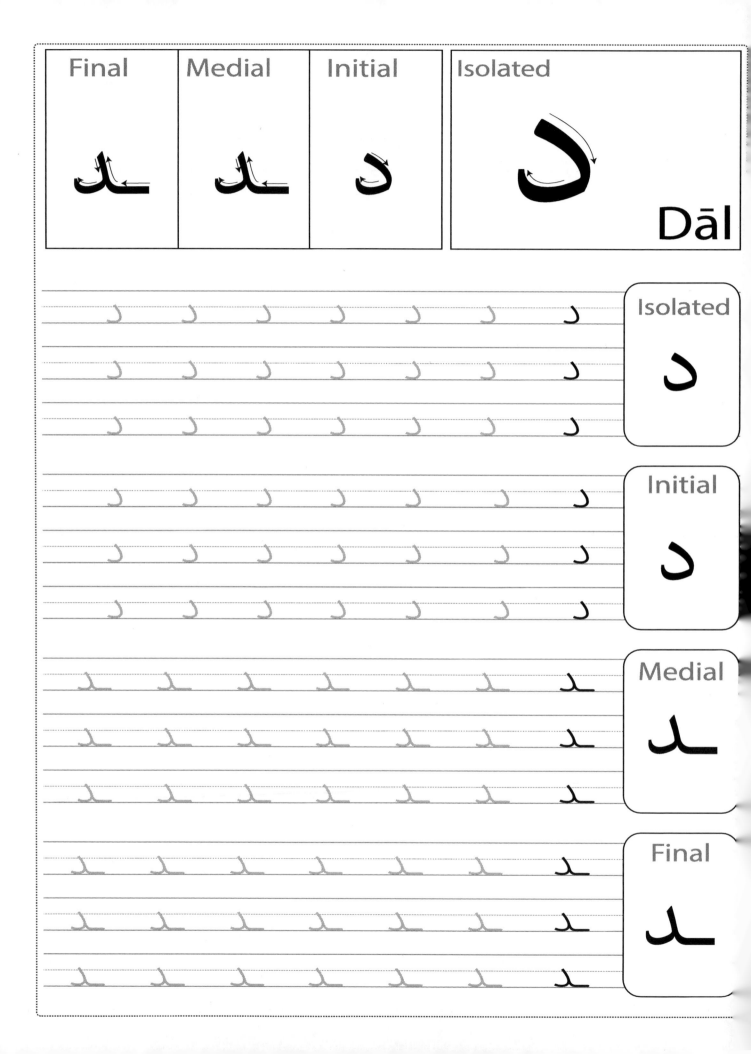

Final	Medial	Initial	Isolated
لـ	ـلـ	د	**Dāl**

Isolated

د

Initial

د

Medial

ـلـ

Final

ـلـ

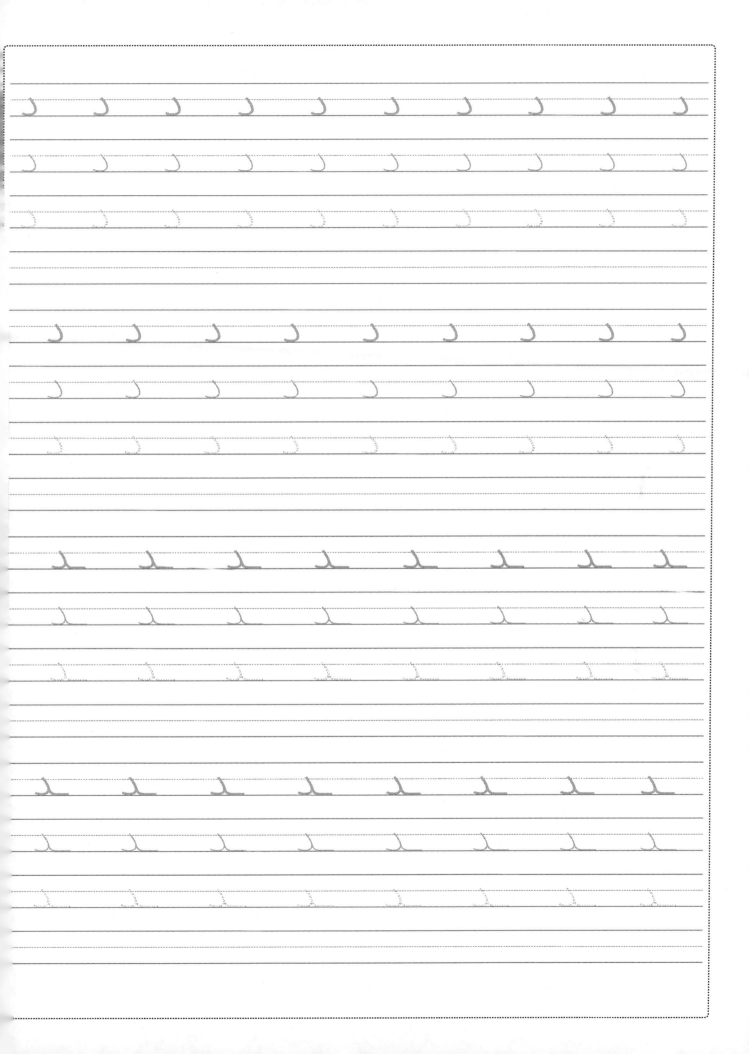

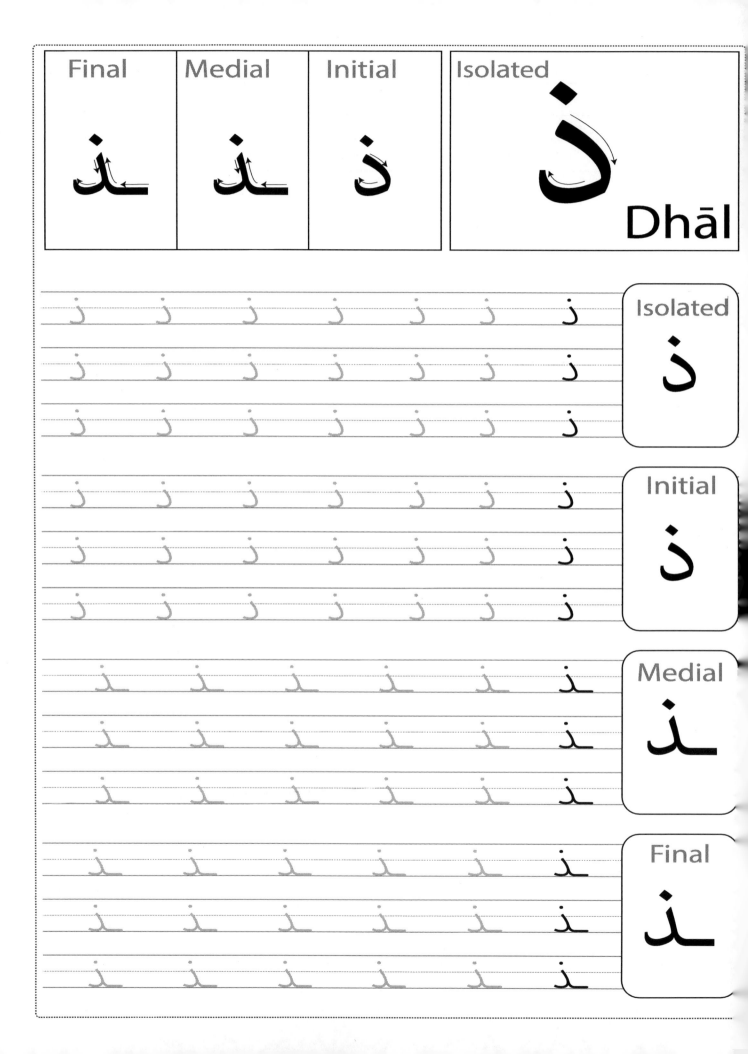

Final	Medial	Initial	Isolated
ـذ	ـذـ	ذ	ذ Dhāl

Isolated
ذ

Initial
ذ

Medial
ـذـ

Final
ـذ

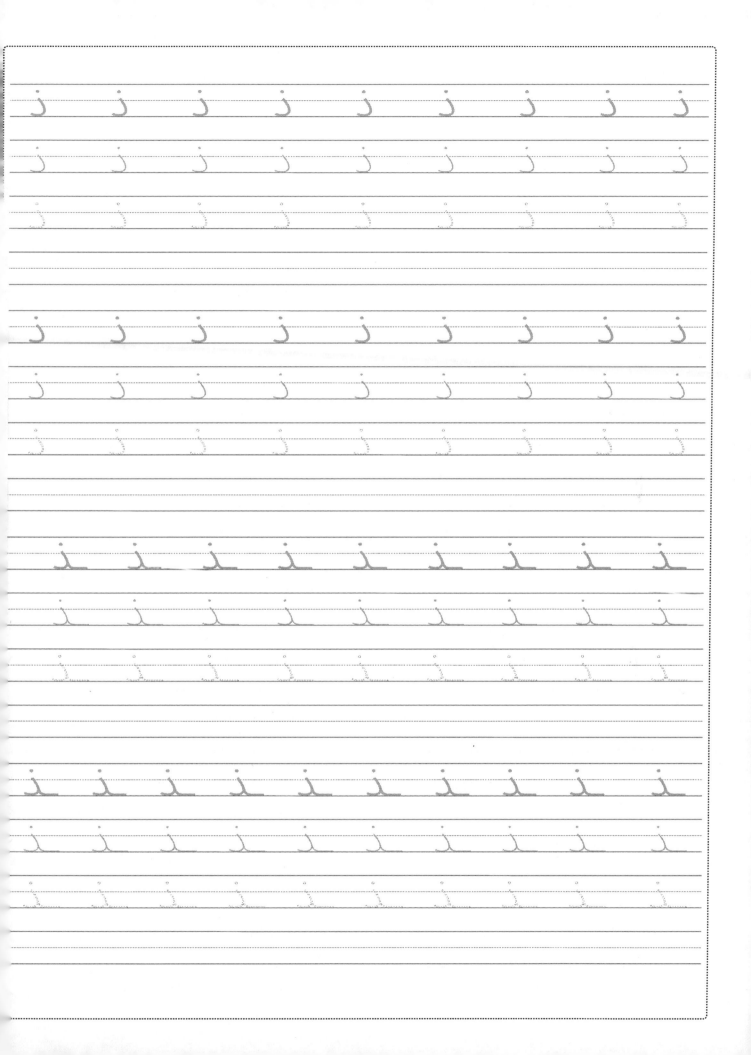

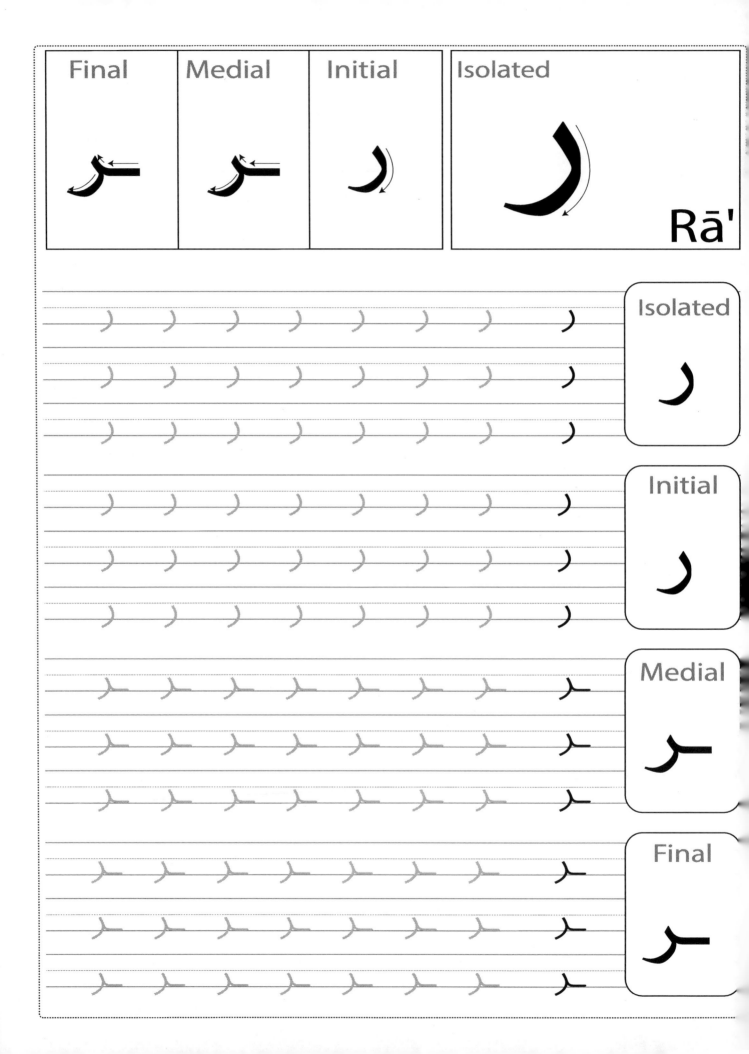

Final	Medial	Initial	Isolated

Rā'

Isolated

Initial

Medial

Final

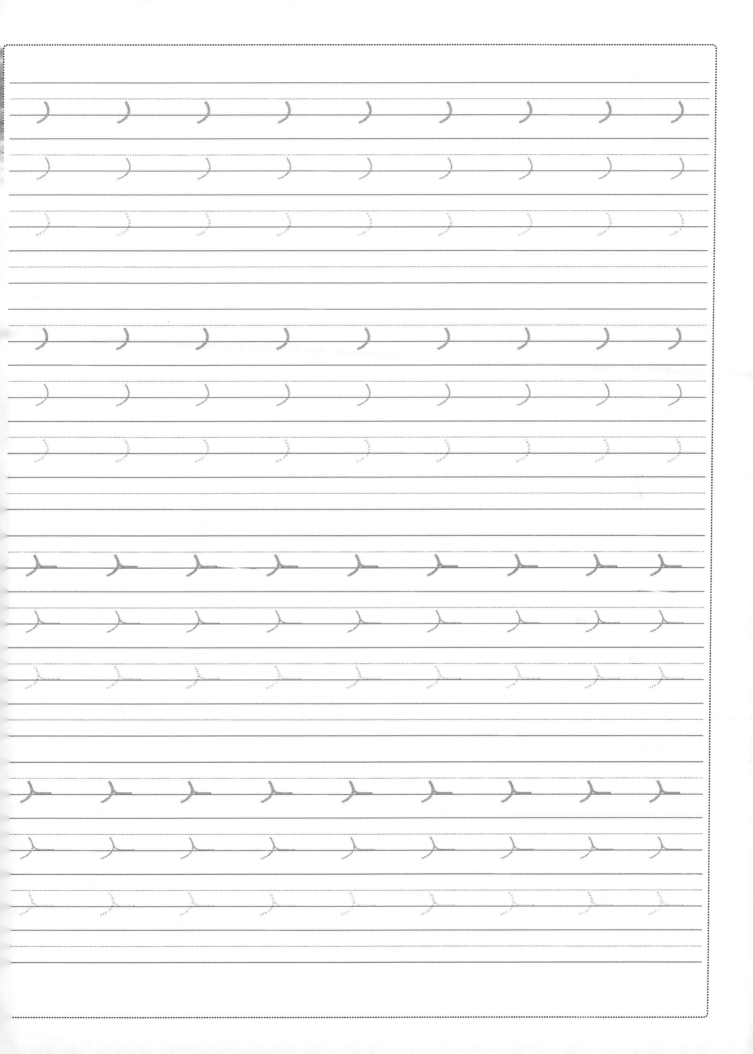

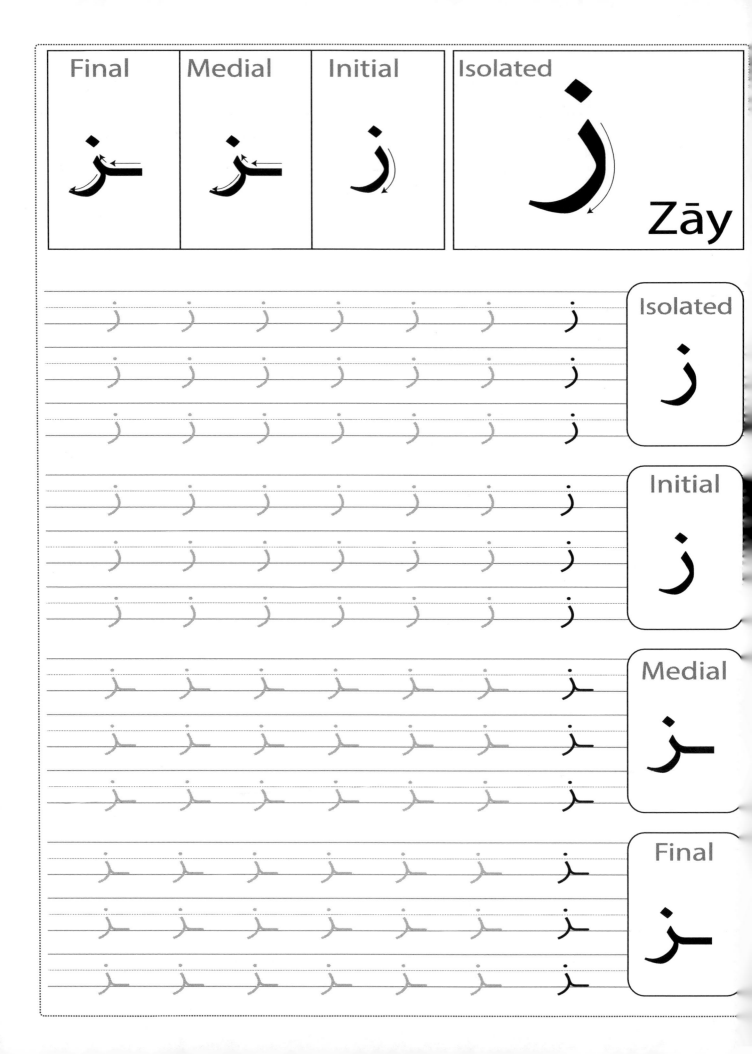

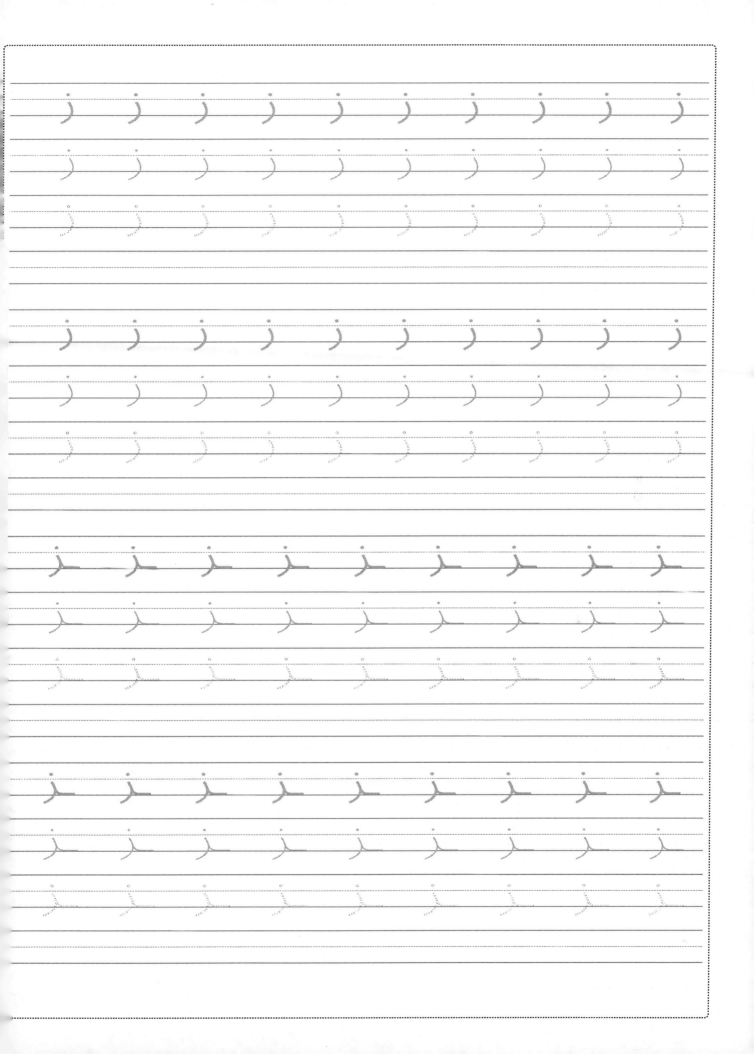

Final	Medial	Initial	Isolated
ـس	ـسـ	سـ	**س** Sīn

Isolated

س

Initial

سـ

Medial

ـسـ

Final

ـس

سس سس سس سس سس سس سس سس سس سس

سس سس سس سس سس سس سس سس سس سس

سس سس سس سس سس سس سس سس سس سس

ست ست ست ست ست ست ست ست ست ست

ست ست ست ست ست ست ست ست ست

بث بث بث بث بث بث بث بث بث بث

ىى ىى ىى ىى ىى ىى ىى ىى ىى ىى

ىى ىى ىى ىى ىى ىى ىى ىى ىى ىى

بى بى بى بى بى بى بى بى

سى سى سى سى سى سى سى سى

سى سى سى سى سى سى سى سى

نثى نثى نثى نثى نثى نثى نثى نثى

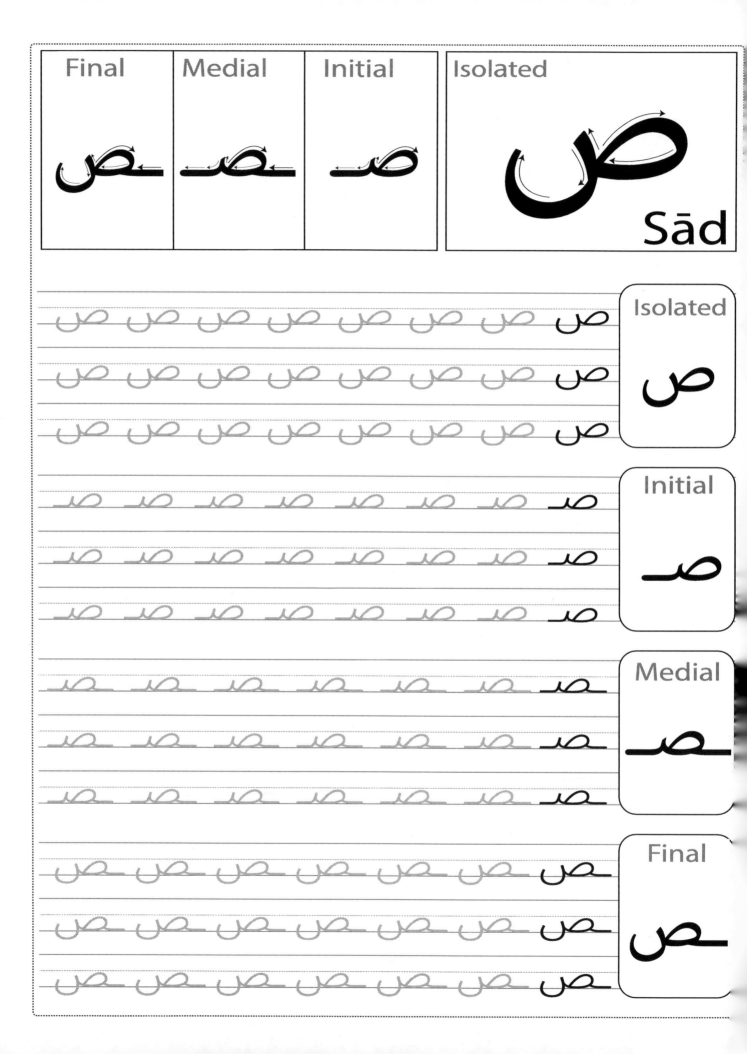

Final	Medial	Initial	Isolated

ص
Sād

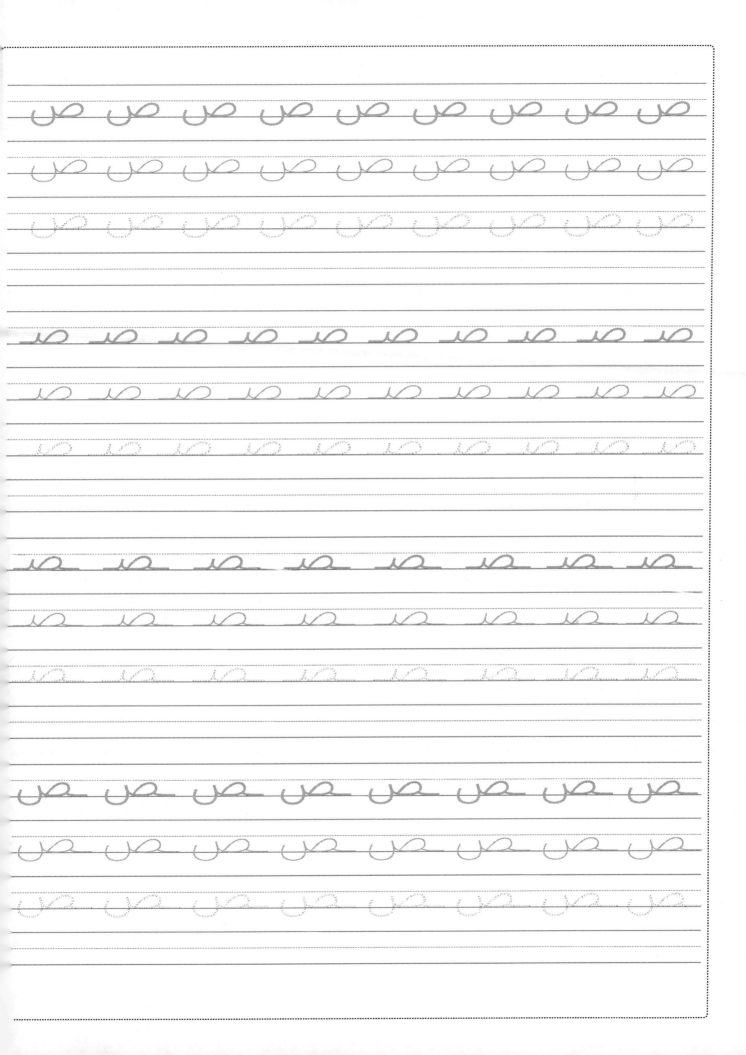

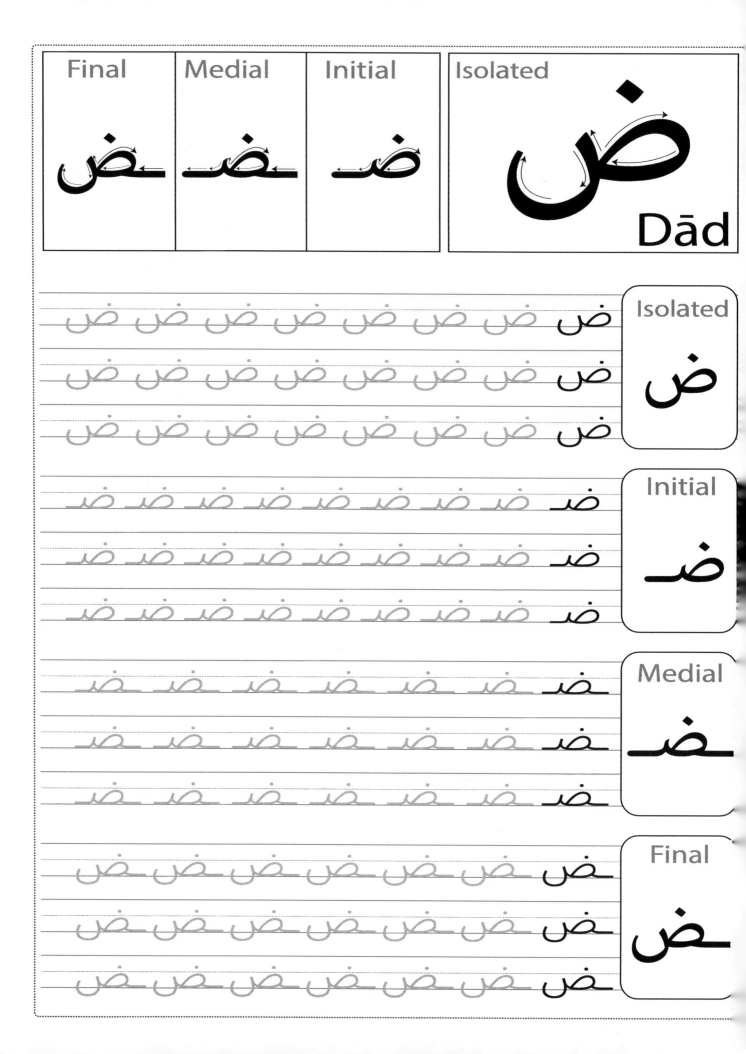

Final	Medial	Initial	Isolated
ض	ض	ض	ض

Dād

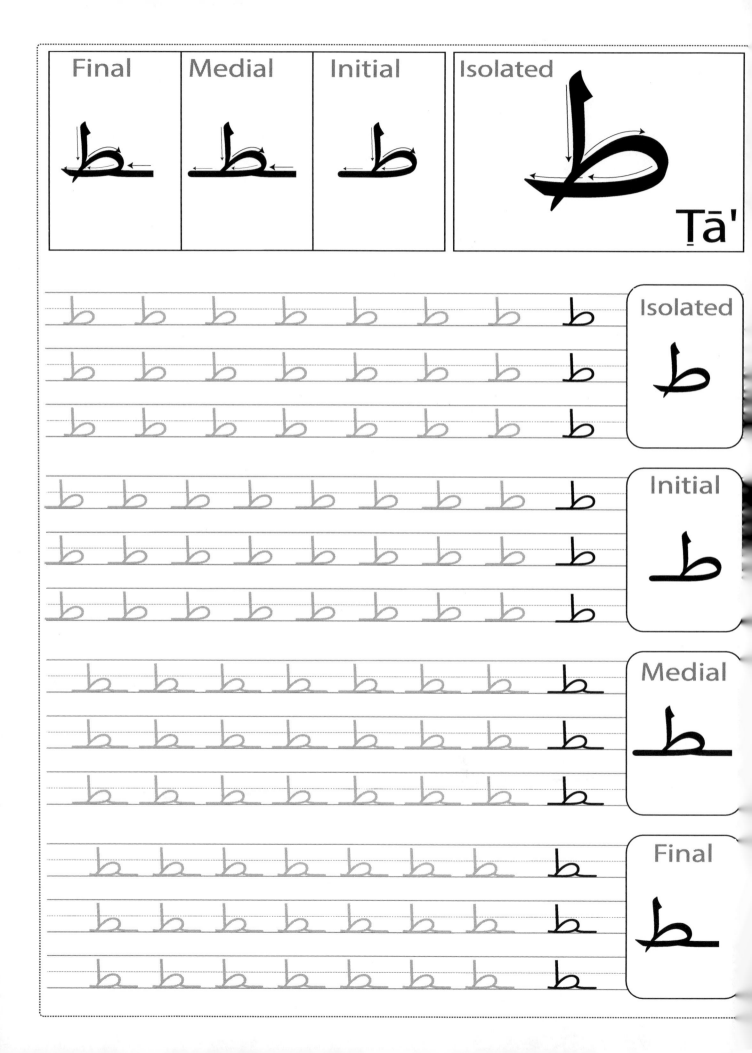

Final	Medial	Initial	Isolated

Ṭā'

Isolated

Initial

Medial

Final

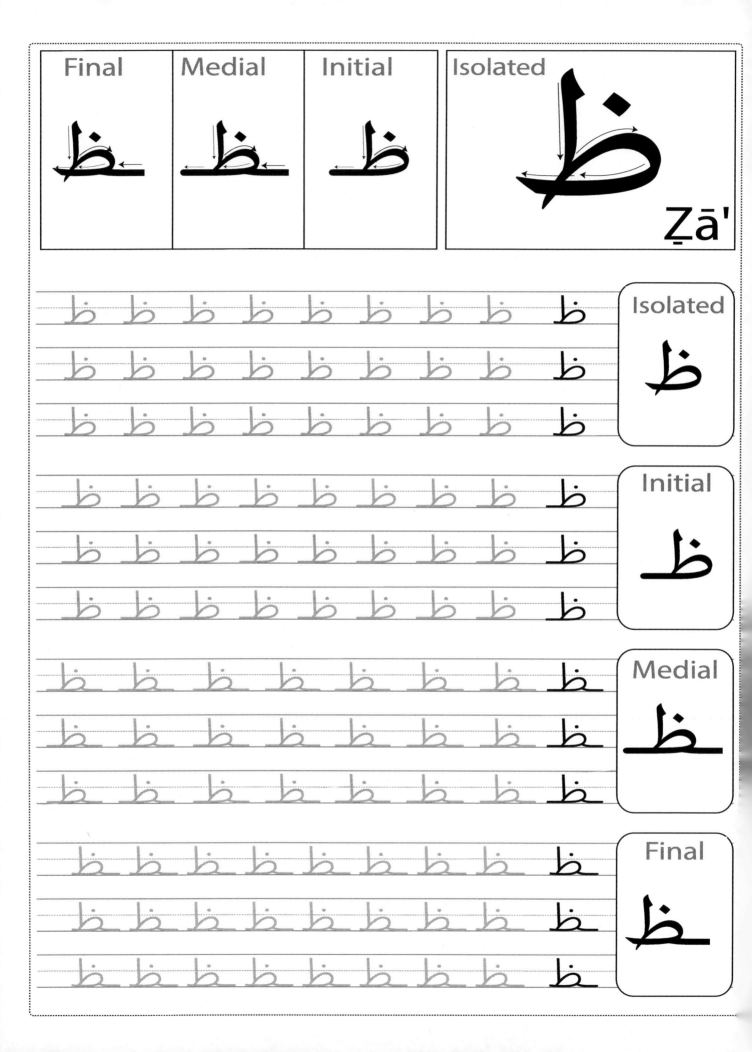

Final	Medial	Initial	Isolated

Ẓā'

Isolated

Initial

Medial

Final

Final	Medial	Initial	Isolated

ع
ʿAin

Isolated
ع

Initial
ع

Medial
ع

Final
ع

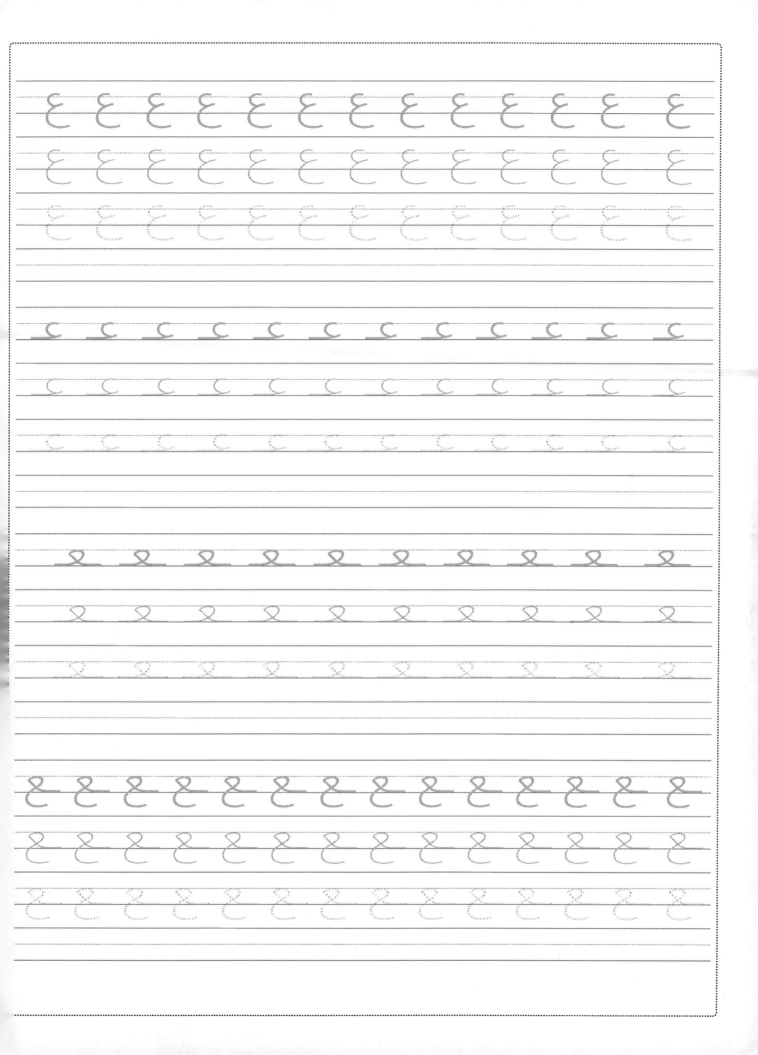

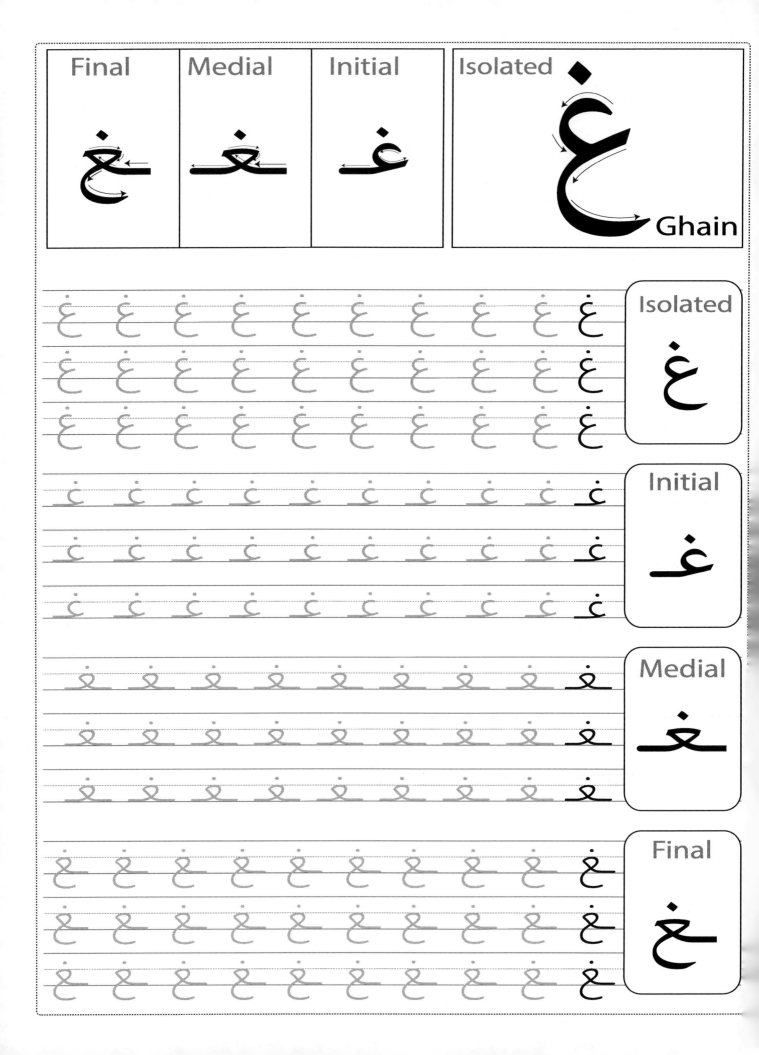

Final	Medial	Initial	Isolated ◆

Ghain

Isolated غ

Initial غـ

Medial ـغـ

Final ـغ

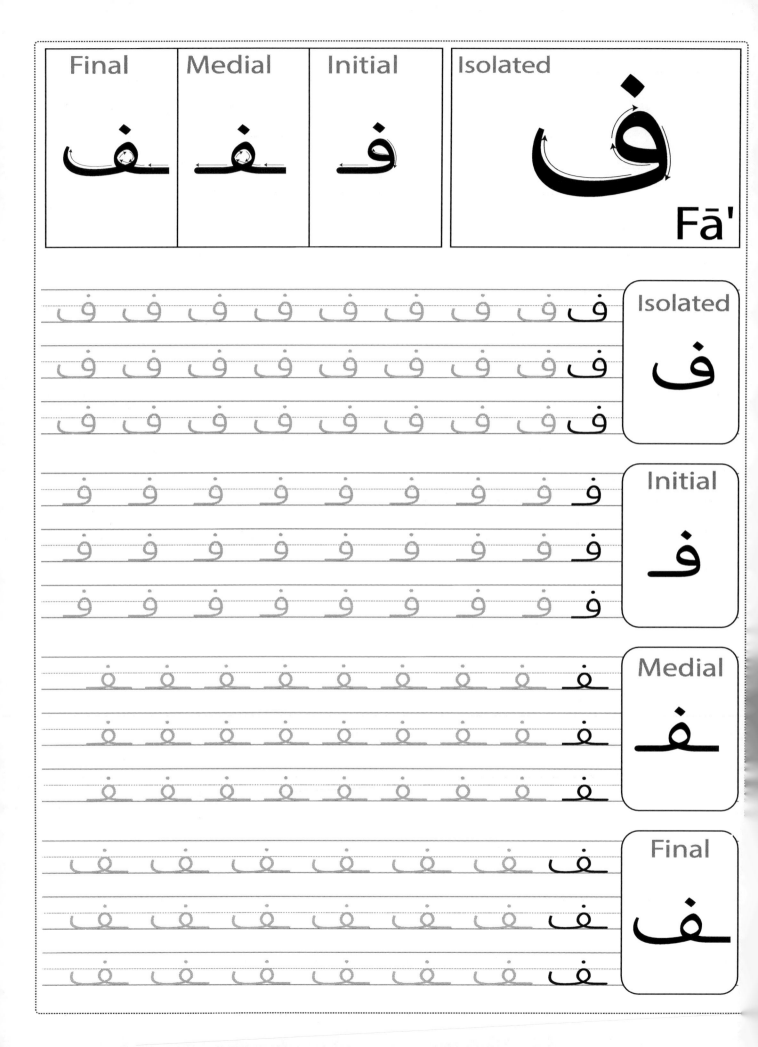

Final	Medial	Initial	Isolated
ف	ف	ف	ف Fā'

	Isolated ف
	Initial ف
	Medial ـفـ
	Final ـف

Final	Medial	Initial	Isolated
ق	ـقـ	قـ	ق Qāf

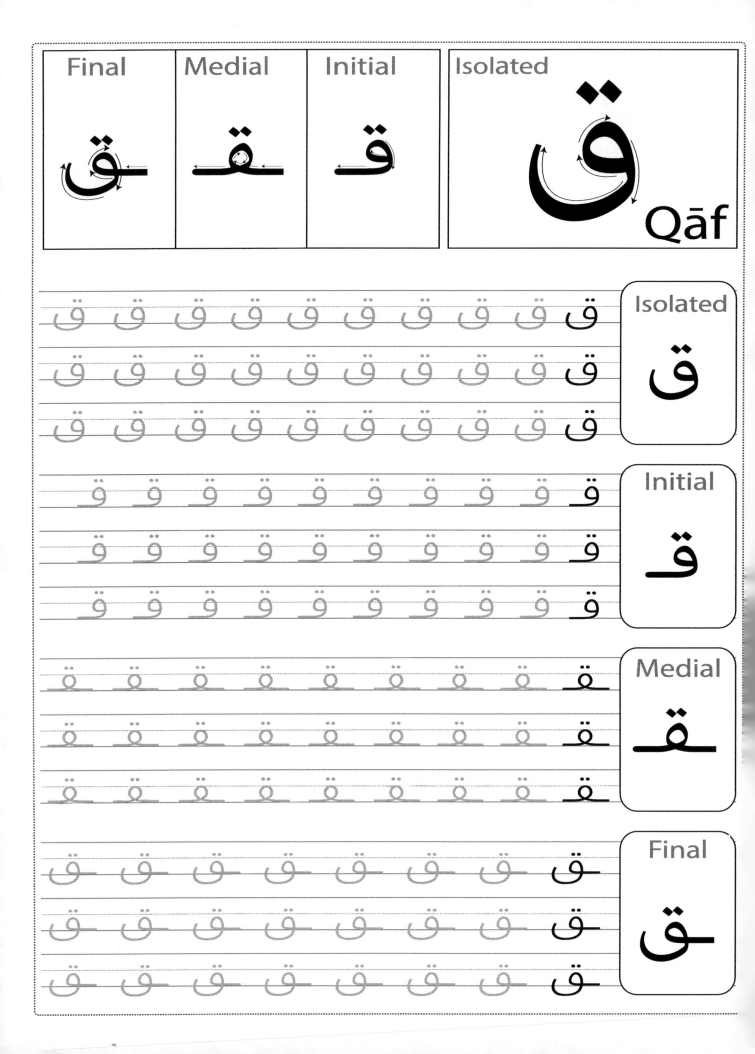

Isolated

ق

Initial

قـ

Medial

ـقـ

Final

ـق

Final	Medial	Initial	Isolated
ك	ـكـ	كـ	ك

Kāf

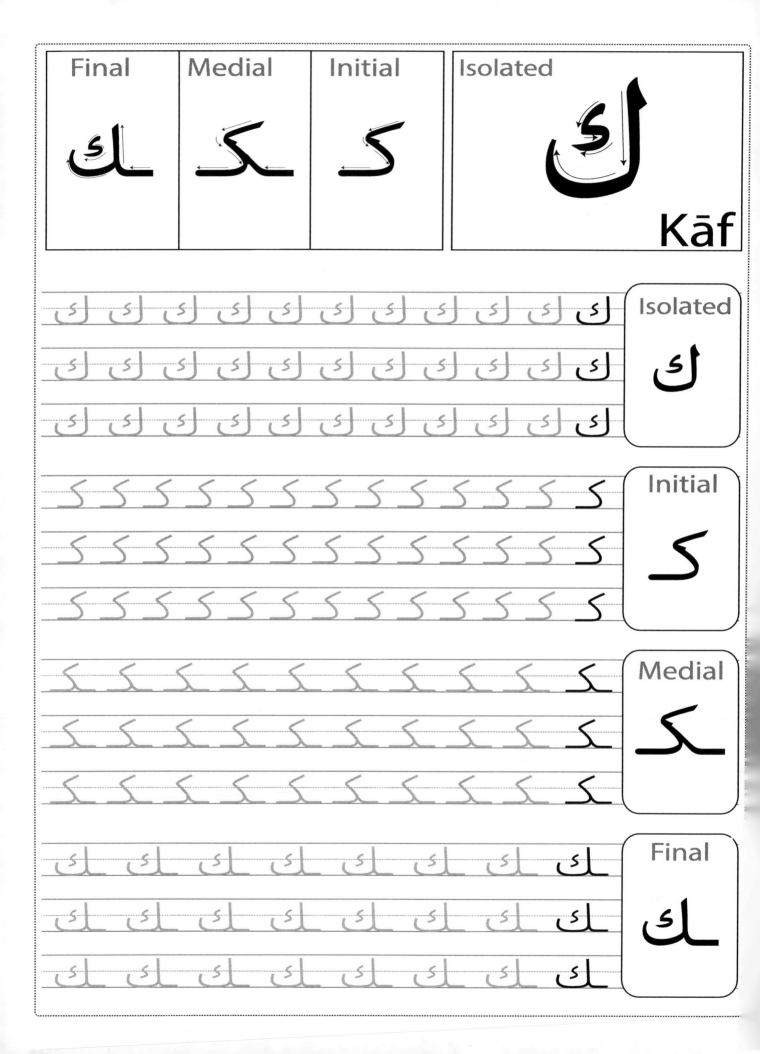

Isolated
ك

Initial
كـ

Medial
ـكـ

Final
ك

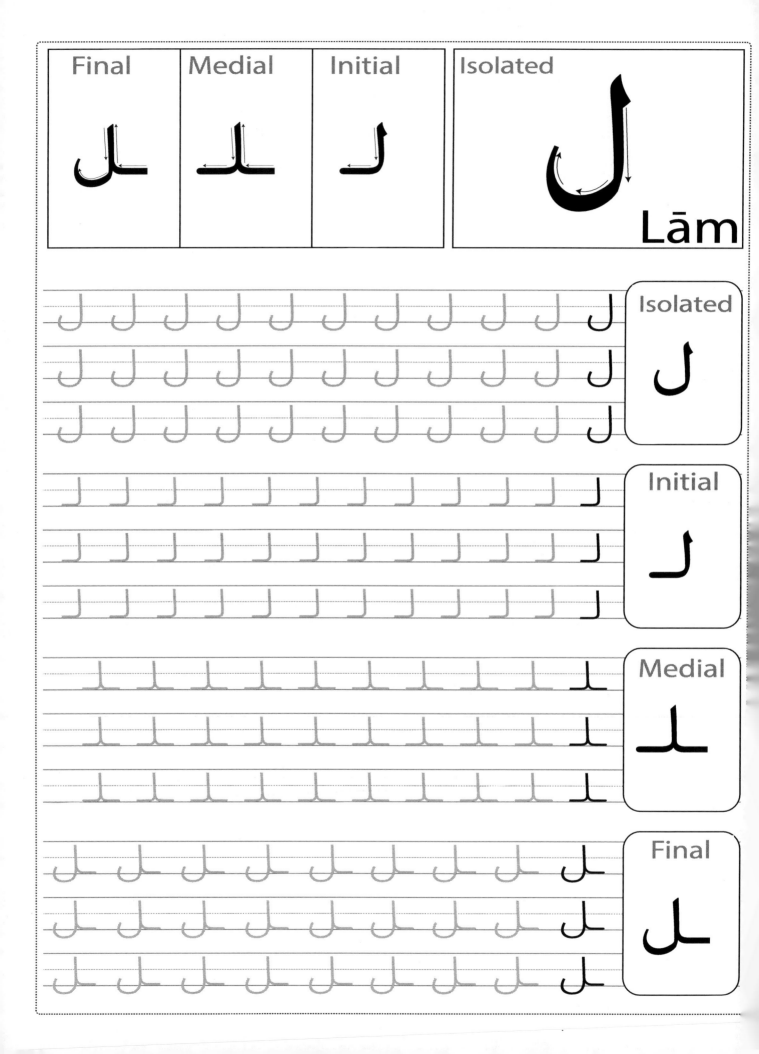

Final	Medial	Initial	Isolated

ل **Lām**

Isolated
ل

Initial
ـل

Medial
ـلـ

Final
ـل

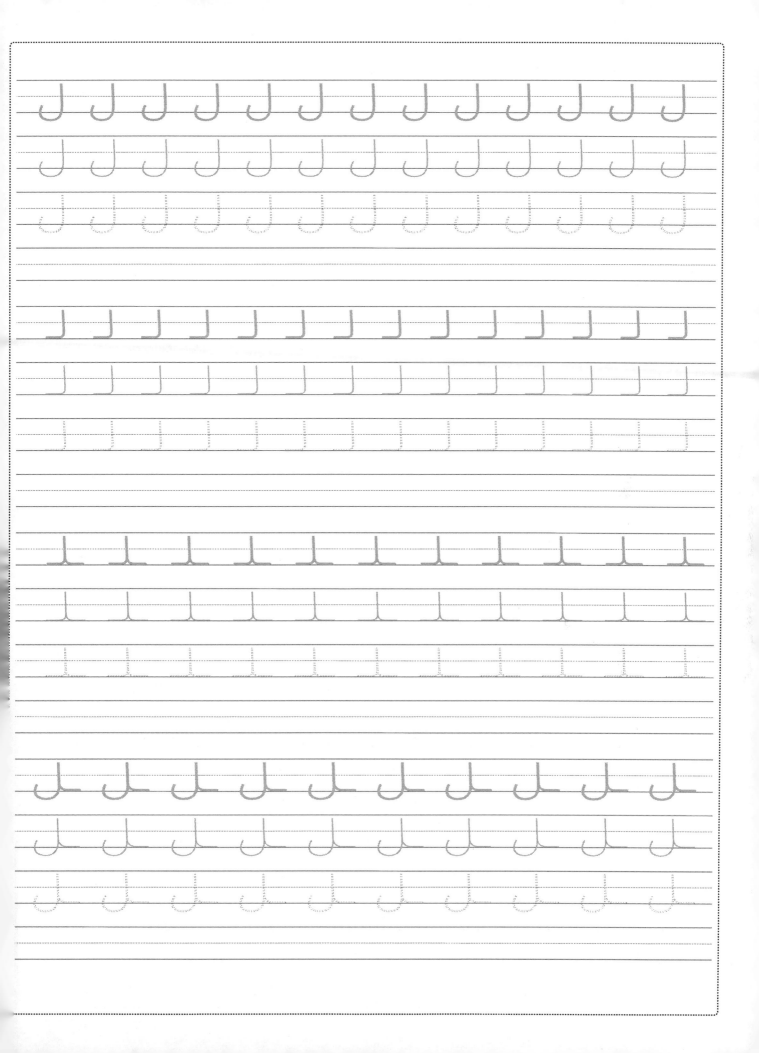

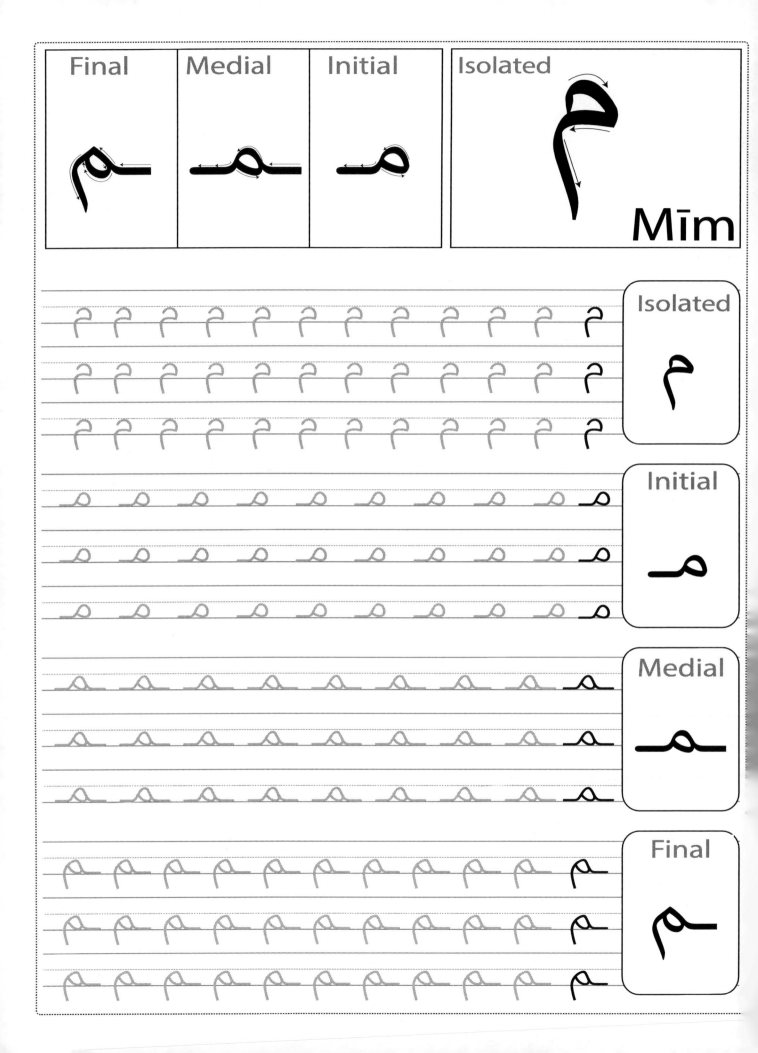

| Final | Medial | Initial | Isolated |

Mīm

Isolated

Initial

Medial

Final

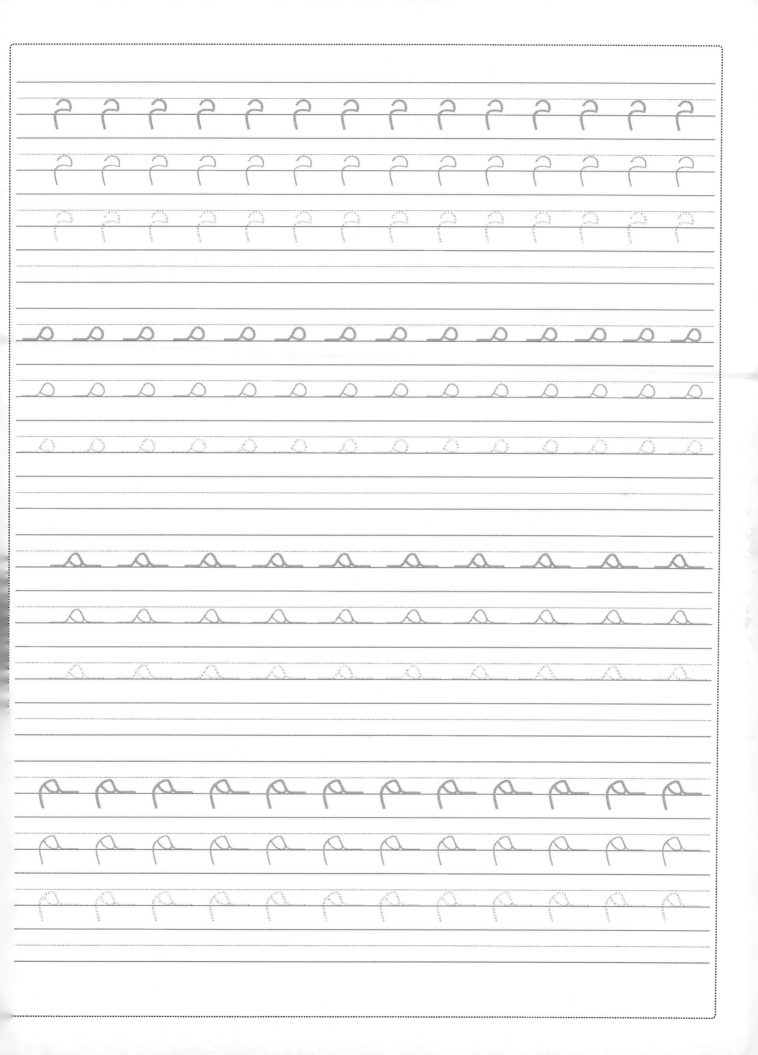

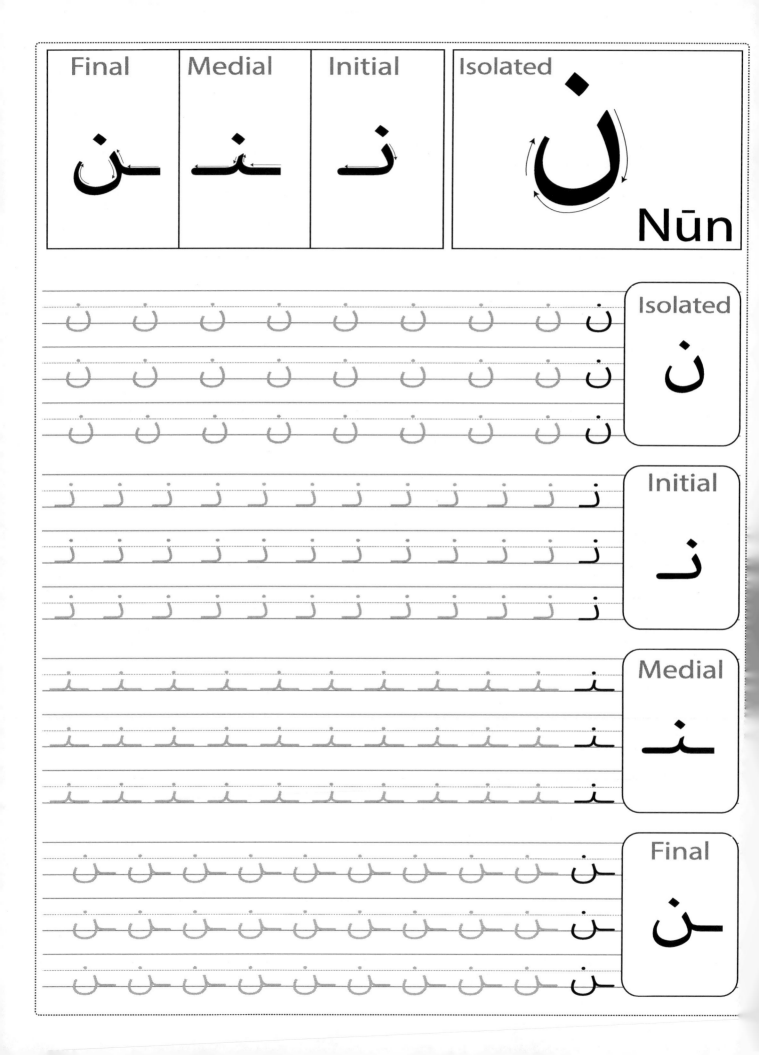

Final	Medial	Initial	Isolated
ـن	ـنـ	نـ	ن

Nūn

Isolated — ن

Initial — نـ

Medial — ـنـ

Final — ـن

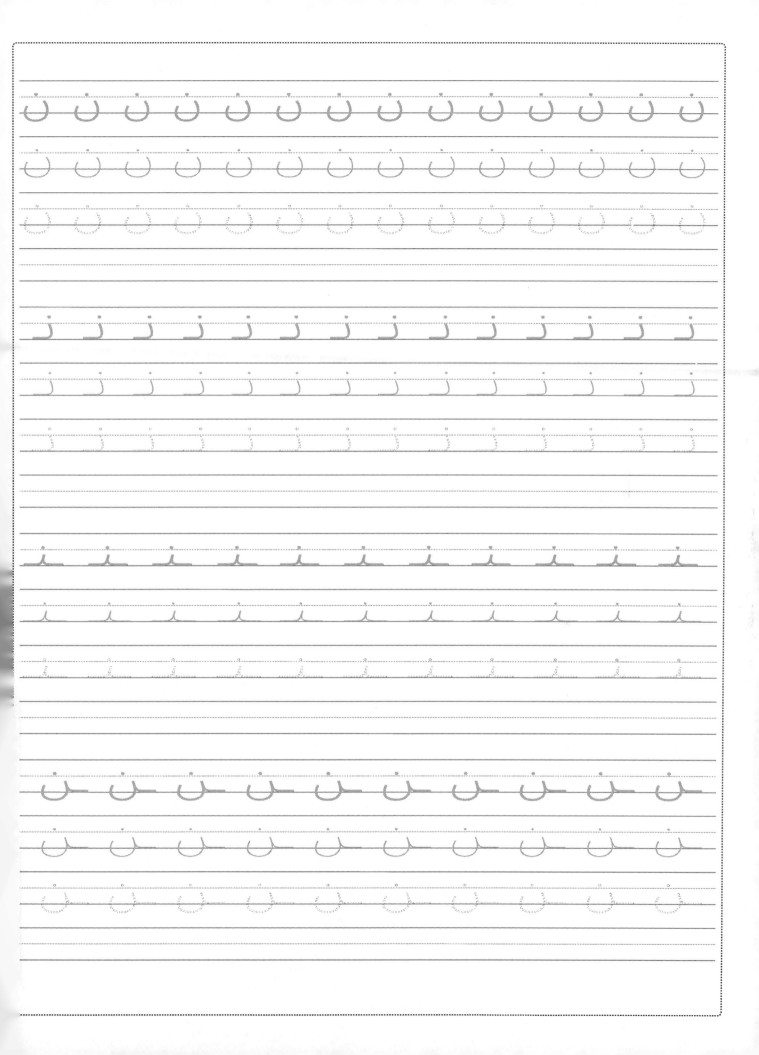

Final	Medial	Initial	Isolated

Hā'

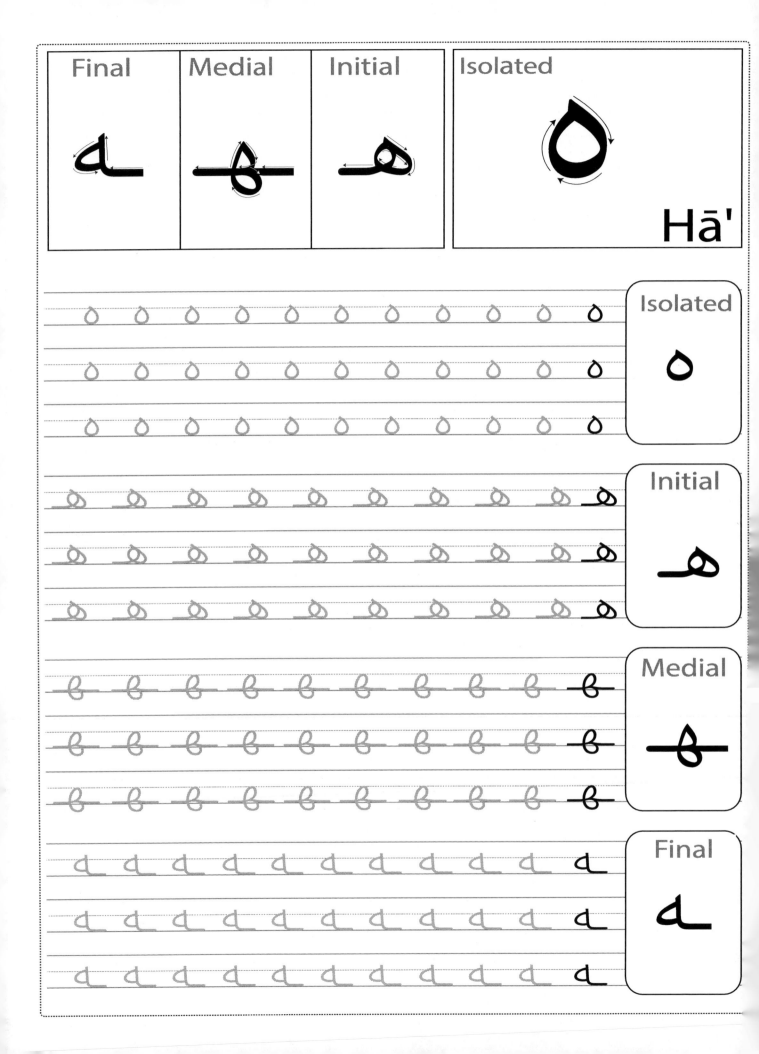

Isolated

Initial

Medial

Final

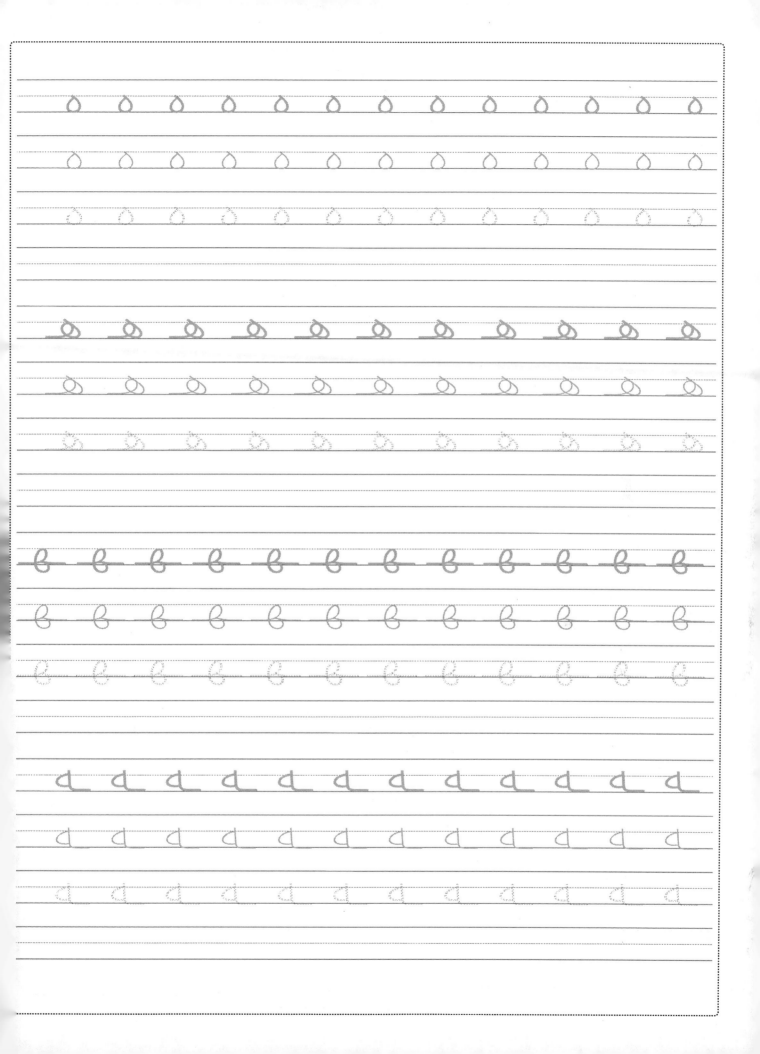

Final	Medial	Initial	Isolated
و	و	و	و

Wāw

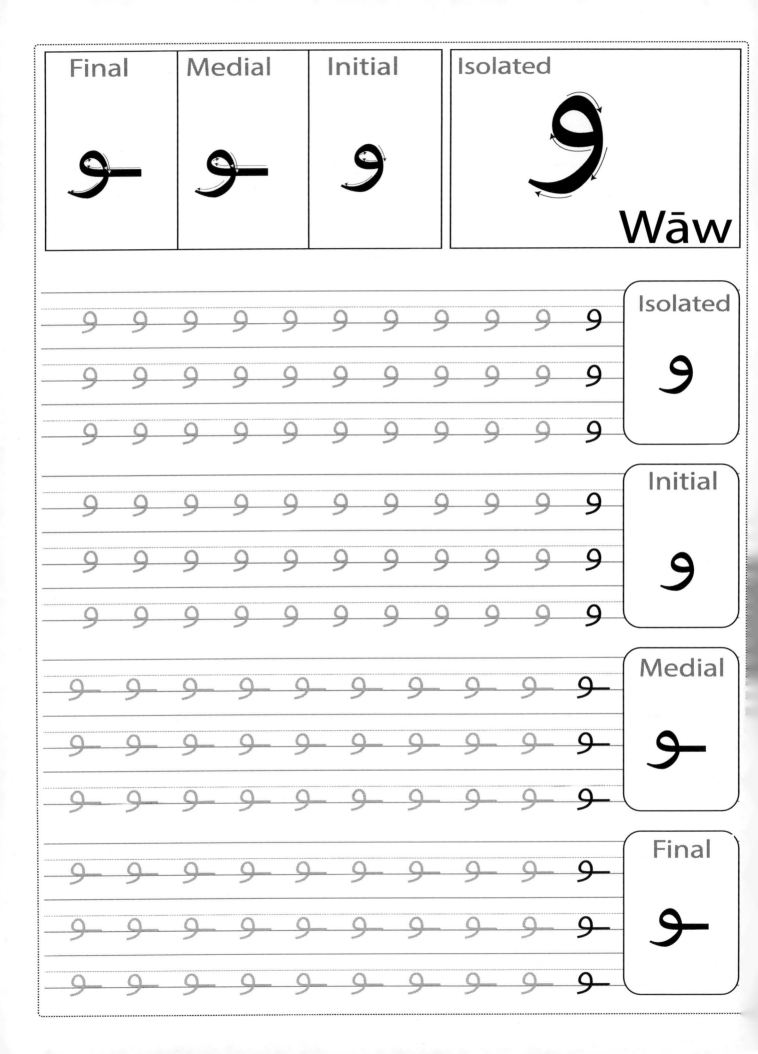

Isolated

و

Initial

و

Medial

و

Final

و

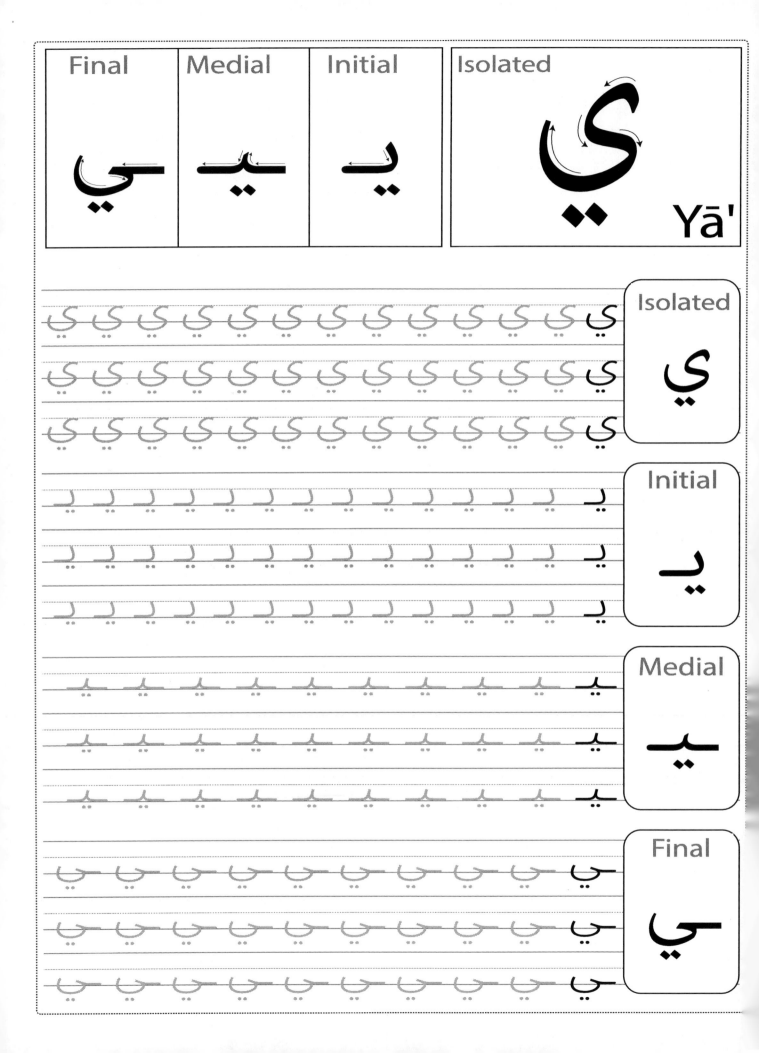

Final	Medial	Initial	Isolated
ـي	ـيـ	يـ	ي Yā'

	Isolated
ي ي ي ي ي ي ي ي ي ي ي ي	ي
ي ي ي ي ي ي ي ي ي ي ي ي	
ي ي ي ي ي ي ي ي ي ي ي ي	

	Initial
يـ يـ يـ يـ يـ يـ يـ يـ يـ يـ يـ يـ	يـ
يـ يـ يـ يـ يـ يـ يـ يـ يـ يـ يـ يـ	
يـ يـ يـ يـ يـ يـ يـ يـ يـ يـ يـ يـ	

	Medial
ـيـ ـيـ ـيـ ـيـ ـيـ ـيـ ـيـ ـيـ ـيـ ـيـ	ـيـ
ـيـ ـيـ ـيـ ـيـ ـيـ ـيـ ـيـ ـيـ ـيـ ـيـ	
ـيـ ـيـ ـيـ ـيـ ـيـ ـيـ ـيـ ـيـ ـيـ ـيـ	

	Final
ـي ـي ـي ـي ـي ـي ـي ـي ـي	ـي
ـي ـي ـي ـي ـي ـي ـي ـي ـي	ي
ـي ـي ـي ـي ـي ـي ـي ـي ـي	

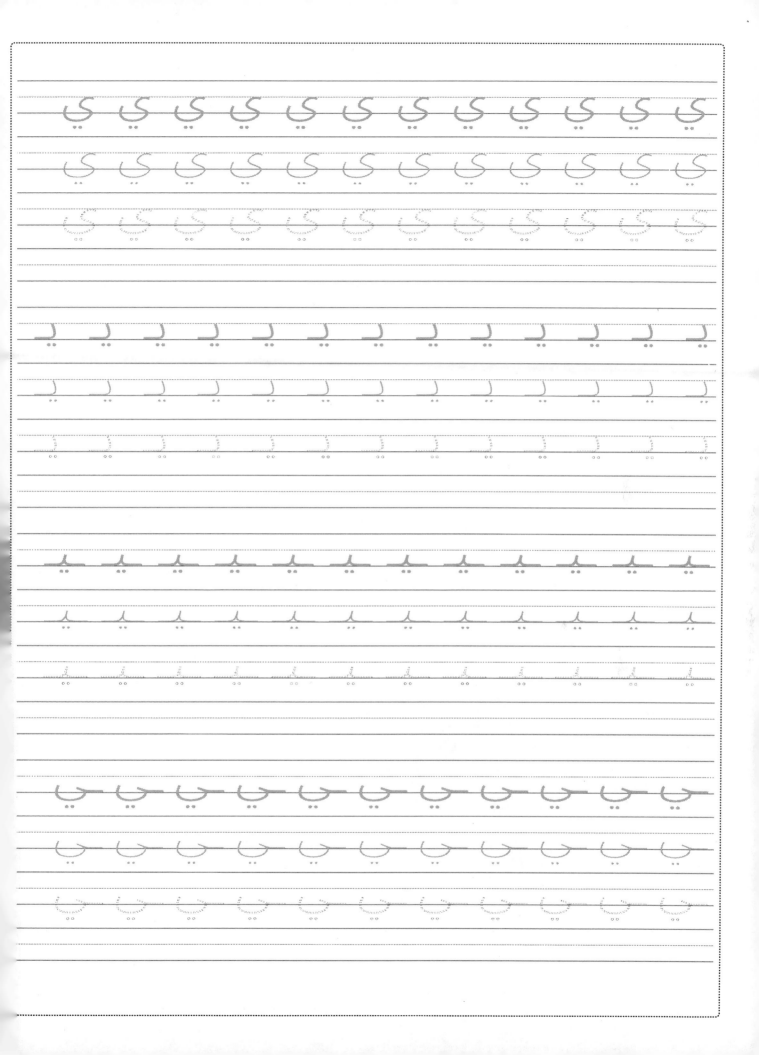

Eastern Arabic numbers الأرقام العربية الشرقية

٠	١	٢	٣	٤
Siffer	Wahid	Ithnan	Thalatha	Arbaâa
0	1	2	3	4
٥	٦	٧	٨	٩
Khamssa	Sitta	Sabäa	Thamaniya	Tissäa
5	6	7	8	9

٤ ٣ ٢ ١ ٠

٩ ٨ ٧ ٦ ٥

Made in the USA
Las Vegas, NV
02 November 2024

11021957R00037